THE COMPLETE COOKBOOK FOR YOUNG CHEFS

Whisk, Stir, Triumph, Young Chef's Handbook for Unforgettable Feasts, Elevate Your Skills, Impress Family & Friends, and Craft Culinary Masterpieces with Ease!

ABBY-JANE BROWN

Abby-Jane Brown © Copyright 2023

All rights reserved.

It is not permitted in any way to reproduce, duplicate, or transmit any part of this document in digital or printed form. Dissemination of this publication is strictly prohibited, and any use of this document is not permitted without the prior written con-sent of the publisher. All rights reserved. The accuracy and integrity of the information contained herein is guaranteed, but no responsibility of any kind is assumed. It is in fact, in terms of misinterpretation of the information through carelessness, or through the use or misuse of any policies, processes, or instructions contained within the book, the sole and absolute responsibility of the intended reader. Under no circumstances may the publisher be legally prosecuted or blamed for any damage done or monetary loss incurred as a result of information contained in this book, either directly or indirectly. Rights are held by the respective authors and not the publisher. Hide these books

Legal Note: This book is copyrighted. It is for personal use only. No part of the contents of this book may be modified, distributed, sold, used, quoted, or paraphrased without the specific consent of the author or copyright owner. Any violation of these terms will be sanctioned as provided by law.

Disclaimer: Please note that the contents of this book are exclusively-for educational and entertainment purposes. Every measure has been taken to provide accurate, up-to-date, and completely reliable information. No warranties of any kind are expressed or implied. Readers acknowledge that the author's opinion is not to be substituted for legal, financial, medical, or professional advice.

INDEX

INTRODUCTION - WELCOME TO THE WORLD OF COOKING: EMBRACING CREATIVITY AND CONFIDENCE 7

CHAPTER 1 - EMBRACING YOUR INNER CHEF 10

'DISCOVERING THE JOY OF COOKING: OVERCOMING SELF-DOUBT AND EMBRACING CULINARY CONFIDENCE' 10

'NURTURING YOUR PASSION: CULTIVATING A LOVE FOR COOKING AT ANY SKILL LEVEL' 12

CHAPTER 2 - SETTING THE FOUNDATION 15

'ESSENTIAL TOOLS AND EQUIPMENT: BUILDING YOUR CULINARY ARSENAL FOR SUCCESS' 15

'MASTERING COOKING TECHNIQUES: FROM SAUTÉING TO BAKING - YOUR GUIDE TO ESSENTIAL SKILLS' 17

CHAPTER 3 - COOKING FOR EVERY OCCASION 20

'WEEKNIGHT WONDERS: QUICK AND EASY RECIPES FOR BUSY YOUNG CHEFS' 20

'FAMILY FEASTS: CREATING MEMORABLE MEALS FOR LOVED ONES' 22

'CELEBRATE WITH FLAIR: SHOWSTOPPING DISHES FOR SPECIAL OCCASIONS' 24

CHAPTER 4 - NAVIGATING CULINARY ADVENTURES 27

'EXPLORING GLOBAL FLAVORS: EMBARKING ON A JOURNEY THROUGH INTERNATIONAL CUISINE'. 27

'CREATIVE FUSION: BLENDING TRADITIONS AND INNOVATIONS IN MODERN COOKING' 29

CHAPTER 5: HEALTHFUL AND WHOLESOME COOKING 32

'FROM FARM TO TABLE: EMBRACING FRESH, SEASONAL INGREDIENTS' 32

'NOURISHING CREATIONS: BALANCING TASTE AND NUTRITION IN EVERY BITE' 34

CHAPTER 6 - THE ART OF BAKING 37

'SWEET SENSATIONS: MASTERING THE BASICS OF BAKING FOR YOUNG PASTRY CHEFS' 37

'BAKING BEYOND THE BASICS: ELEVATING YOUR DESSERTS TO THE NEXT LEVEL' 39

CHAPTER 7 - KITCHEN CONFIDENCE AND BEYOND 42

'OVERCOMING KITCHEN DISASTERS: TURNING MISTAKES INTO LEARNING OPPORTUNITIES' 42

'SHARING THE LOVE: COOKING FOR FRIENDS, FAMILY, AND BEYOND' 44

CHAPTER 8 47

BREAKFAST RECIPES 47

CHAPTER 9 .... *55*

LUNCH RECIPES *55*

CHAPTER 10 .... *62*

DINNER RECIPES *62*

CHAPTER 11 .... *71*

SNACKS RECIPES *71*

CHAPTER 12 - BUILDING A CULINARY LEGACY *78*

'CAPTURING MEMORIES: DOCUMENTING YOUR CULINARY JOURNEY AND CREATIONS' 78

'PASSING ON THE PASSION: INSPIRING OTHERS TO EMBRACE THE ART OF COOKING'....................81

CHAPTER 13 - REAL STORIES, REAL CHEFS *85*

'INSPIRING JOURNEYS: STORIES OF YOUNG CHEFS WHO OVERCAME CHALLENGES AND FOUND SUCCESS' 85

'CONNECTING THROUGH COOKING: BUILDING A COMMUNITY OF YOUNG CULINARY ENTHUSIASTS' 88

CHAPTER 14 - YOUR CULINARY ADVENTURE AWAITS *92*

'BEYOND THE BOOK: EXPLORING FURTHER RESOURCES, BLOGS, AND ONLINE COMMUNITIES'.......92

'CULINARY EXPLORATION: EMBARKING ON NEW ADVENTURES IN THE WORLD OF COOKING'........95

CONCLUSION - EMBRACING YOUR ROLE AS A YOUNG CHEF: LOOKING BACK AND MOVING FORWARD WITH CONFIDENCE *99*

Here is as promised the free bonus, all you have to do is scan the QR CODE and follow the steps and in less than a minute you will receive the bonus!

INTRODUCTION

WELCOME TO THE WORLD OF COOKING: EMBRACING CREATIVITY AND CONFIDENCE

INTRODUCTION - WELCOME TO THE WORLD OF COOKING: EMBRACING CREATIVITY AND CONFIDENCE

Welcome to a world filled with excitement, flavor, and magic – the enchanting world of cooking! Just like a brave explorer embarking on a thrilling journey, you're about to uncover the mysteries of the kitchen. Get ready to discover new tastes, create delicious meals, and become a young chef with confidence.

Think of the kitchen as your very own playground, where ingredients are your toys and recipes are your adventures. Every dish you create is like a masterpiece, painted with colors of flavors and seasoned with your creativity. From sizzling pans to aromatic spices, the kitchen is a place where wonders happen.

Imagine whisking eggs into a frothy frenzy to make fluffy pancakes that dance on your plate. Picture sprinkling cheese on a pizza and watching it melt into a gooey delight. As a young chef, you have the power to turn simple ingredients into extraordinary feasts that make your taste buds dance.

But cooking isn't just about making food – it's about embracing your imagination and expressing yourself. Just like an artist uses paint and canvas, you use ingredients and utensils to craft your culinary art. Whether you're flipping pancakes or stirring a simmering pot of soup, every move you make is a stroke of your cooking brush.

And guess what? You don't need to be a grown-up to create mouthwatering dishes. Cooking is for everyone, including young chefs like you! With a dash of curiosity and a sprinkle of enthusiasm, you're ready to conquer the kitchen. And here's a little secret: even the most famous chefs started right where you are, taking their first steps in the world of flavors and aromas.

In this book, you'll find all sorts of secrets and tricks that will make your cooking adventures even more exciting. From understanding different ingredients to mastering cooking techniques, each page holds a treasure trove of knowledge to unlock. And as you follow along with the recipes, you'll learn how to whip up breakfasts that brighten your mornings, lunches that give you energy, snacks that satisfy your cravings, and dinners that bring joy to your evenings.

But cooking isn't just about following recipes – it's about experimenting, trying new things, and making each dish your own. Just like an inventor tinkering in a lab, you can mix and match flavors, add your special twist, and create something entirely unique. So go ahead, be bold and daring in your kitchen adventures!

Remember, every time you cook, you're not just making food. You're creating memories, bonding with family and friends, and nourishing both your body and your soul. So get ready to step into the wonderful world of cooking, where every ingredient is a story waiting to be told, and every recipe is a journey to savor.

Are you excited? Great! The journey is about to begin. Get ready to chop, stir, mix, and sprinkle your way to becoming a young chef who knows no limits. So put on your apron, tie up your chef's hat, and let's dive into the enchanting world of cooking together!

CHAPTER 1

EMBRACING YOUR INNER CHEF

CHAPTER 1 - EMBRACING YOUR INNER CHEF

'DISCOVERING THE JOY OF COOKING: OVERCOMING SELF-DOUBT AND EMBRACING CULINARY CONFIDENCE'

Cooking is like a magic potion – it's a mix of fun, adventure, and deliciousness! But sometimes, a tiny voice inside our heads says, "Can I really do this?" It's called self-doubt, and guess what? Everyone feels it, even the greatest chefs out there. But here's the best part: you have the power to overcome it and become a confident young chef!

Imagine you're a superhero in your kitchen, with a cape made of apron strings. When you put on that apron, you transform into a culinary wizard who can create amazing dishes. Sure, you might wonder if your pancakes will flip perfectly or if your cookies will be too crunchy, but here's the secret: mistakes are like secret ingredients in your cooking adventure.

Just like a treasure hunt, cooking is all about exploring, trying new things, and having a blast along the way. You might mix up salt and sugar by accident or spill flour like fairy dust, but guess what? Those little mishaps are what make your cooking journey unique and exciting.

You're on a cooking show, and you're the star chef. As you chop veggies and stir sauces, you're not just making food – you're telling a story. Your kitchen becomes a stage where flavors dance and ingredients sing. And guess who's in control of this delicious play? You!

So, how can you overcome self-doubt and become the fearless chef you're meant to be? Start by believing in yourself! Just like a superhero believes they can save the day, you can believe in your cooking powers. Every time you try a new recipe, you're adding a new skill to your chef's toolkit.

It's okay if your cookies turn out a little lopsided or if your pasta is a tad too soft. Every culinary adventure is a chance to learn, grow, and get better. Remember, even the most famous chefs had their share of cooking mishaps before they became culinary legends.

And here's a secret tip from the kitchen: when you cook with love and excitement, your dishes taste even better! Your joy gets mixed right into the recipe, and it's like a sprinkle of magic that makes everything delicious.

The next time you hear that tiny voice of doubt, tell it, "I've got this!" Put on your apron, gather your ingredients, and dive into your cooking adventure. With every whisk, every stir, and every sizzle, you're becoming a more confident young chef.

Cooking is your chance to shine like a star, to create masterpieces that make your taste buds dance, and to share the joy of food with everyone around you. So, embrace your culinary powers, and remember that every time you step into the kitchen, you're not just cooking – you're crafting joy, confidence, and delicious memories!

Now, put on your chef's hat and let's conquer the kitchen together! Your cooking adventure is waiting, and guess what? You've got all the ingredients for success!

'NURTURING YOUR PASSION: CULTIVATING A LOVE FOR COOKING AT ANY SKILL LEVEL'

Imagine your kitchen as a magical garden, where ingredients are like seeds waiting to grow into delicious wonders. Just like a gardener tends to their plants, you can nurture your love for cooking and watch it bloom into something truly amazing. No matter if you're a beginner or a young chef with some experience, there's always room to cultivate your passion for cooking!

Think of cooking as a grand adventure, where you're the fearless explorer and the recipe is your treasure map. Whether you're mixing batter for fluffy cupcakes or sautéing veggies for a stir-fry, every moment in the kitchen is a chance to discover, learn, and create.

But how do you nurture your love for cooking, you ask? It's simple – start with something you're curious about. Maybe you've always wondered how cookies get their chocolatey goodness or how spaghetti magically turns tender when boiled. Curiosity is like the water that helps your culinary passion grow!

Just like a puzzle, cooking is about putting pieces together to create something amazing. You start with ingredients, mix in a pinch of creativity, follow a recipe like a map, and voila – you've created a masterpiece! And the best part? You can adjust the puzzle pieces to make your creation uniquely yours.

Let's talk about flavors – they're like colors on your palette. Just like an artist mixes colors to create beautiful paintings, you can mix flavors to create incredible dishes. Add a squeeze of lemon to make things zesty, a sprinkle of herbs to make them aromatic, and a dash of love to make them truly special.

But the most important thing is that there is no correct or incorrect way of cooking! You are master of the crew and guide the helm in your own kitchen! You decide what touch to give to your recipes.

Cooking is like a game where everyone wins. Even if your cupcakes don't rise perfectly or your pasta turns a little soft, you're still a champion for trying! Every time you cook, you're learning something new and growing as a young chef.

Here's a secret: you don't need to be a grown-up to create amazing dishes. Just like a flower needs sunlight to bloom, your cooking needs your love and attention. The more you cook, the more you'll fall in love with the process – the sizzle of a pan, the aroma of spices, and the joy of creating something delicious.

So, grab your apron and embark on a journey to nurture your cooking passion. Explore new recipes, experiment with flavors, and most importantly, have fun! Whether you're making a simple sandwich or a fancy dessert, every dish you create is a step closer to becoming a culinary superstar.

Remember, cooking is about joy, creativity, and sharing something special with the people you care about. So, let your passion for cooking grow like a beautiful garden, and watch as it fills your kitchen with love and deliciousness. Your cooking adventure awaits – let's nurture your culinary dreams together!

CHAPTER 2

SETTING THE FOUNDATION

CHAPTER 2 - SETTING THE FOUNDATION

'ESSENTIAL TOOLS AND EQUIPMENT: BUILDING YOUR CULINARY ARSENAL FOR SUCCESS'

Picture your kitchen as a magical workshop, and the tools and equipment are your trusty sidekicks. Just like a superhero's gadgets, these tools help you conquer culinary challenges and create delicious wonders. From spatulas that flip like acrobats to mixing bowls that dance with ingredients, every tool has a special role in your kitchen adventure.

First up, let's talk about knives – they're like the knights of your culinary castle. With a well-sharpened knife, you can chop veggies, slice fruits, and cut ingredients into perfect shapes. Just remember to be super careful and always ask an adult for help when using sharp knives.

Next, say hello to your measuring cups and spoons – they're like the treasure chests of precise cooking. They help you measure ingredients so that your recipes turn out just right. Whether it's flour for fluffy pancakes or sugar for sweet treats, measuring is like a secret potion that ensures your dishes taste amazing.

Now, let's meet your mixing buddies – the bowls and spoons that work together like a musical symphony. When you're baking cookies or whipping up pancake batter, these tools make sure everything gets mixed evenly, creating a harmonious blend of flavors.

And what about the pots and pans? They're like the stages where your ingredients perform their delicious dances. Whether you're sautéing veggies or simmering soups, pots and pans help you cook your ingredients to perfection, making every dish a culinary masterpiece.

Just like an artist needs a canvas, you need cutting boards to create your edible artworks. These colorful boards keep your ingredients safe and your kitchen tidy. Plus, they're great for chopping, slicing, and dicing without making a mess.

Let's not forget about the oven and stovetop – they're like the magical portals that turn raw ingredients into mouthwatering delights. When you bake cookies, roast veggies, or cook pasta, these tools work their enchantment, transforming your creations into tasty wonders.

Oh, and have you met the mixing bowls and whisks? They're like the dancers of your culinary ballet. When you're making fluffy batters or creamy dressings, these tools twirl and swirl, mixing ingredients with finesse and flair.

Now, let's talk about measuring scales – they're like the wizards of precision. They help you weigh ingredients accurately, especially for recipes that need precise measurements, like baking cakes or making bread.

Last but not least, the blender and food processor are like your kitchen magicians. They blend, chop, and puree ingredients to create smoothies, sauces, and dips. These are the tools you need to add some imagination to your kitchen!

Each tool in your kitchen arsenal has a special role in your culinary adventure. Just like a superhero's powers, these tools help you create delicious dishes that make everyone smile. But above all, it is you who directs the work, you decide the magic to do, so roll up your sleeves and start to bear fruit to your imagination in the kitchen. With every chop, stir, and sizzle, you're becoming a culinary superstar. Happy cooking, young chef – your culinary journey is full of delicious possibilities!

'MASTERING COOKING TECHNIQUES: FROM SAUTÉING TO BAKING - YOUR GUIDE TO ESSENTIAL SKILLS'

Cooking is like a secret code – once you unlock the right techniques, you become a culinary wizard who can create delicious spells in the kitchen. From sizzling to baking, each technique is like a magical tool that helps you create incredible dishes. So, let's dive into the world of cooking techniques and become young chefs who can cook up a storm!

First up, sautéing – it's like a dance your ingredients do in a hot pan. When you sauté, you toss veggies or meat in a pan with a bit of oil. They sizzle, dance, and turn golden and delicious. It's like giving your ingredients a quick, exciting workout!

Then there's baking – it's like a hug from the oven. When you bake, you pop dishes into the oven and let them transform into mouthwatering delights. Whether it's cookies that go from dough to golden treats or cakes that rise like magic, baking is like creating edible wonders.

Grilling is like a little barbecue party in your kitchen. You place ingredients on a hot grill or a grill pan, and they get those awesome grill marks and a delicious smoky flavor. It's like adding a taste of adventure to your dishes!

Boiling is like a cozy bath for your ingredients. When you boil, you cook things in hot water until they become tender and delicious. It's like turning hard pasta into soft noodles or making veggies just right for munching.

Stir-frying is like a super-speedy cooking adventure. You use high heat and quick movements to cook ingredients in a hot pan. It's like creating a flavor-packed stir-fry that's ready in a flash!

And then there's steaming – it's like a gentle hug for your food. When you steam, you cook ingredients by letting steam do the magic. It's like creating a healthy and delicious dish without needing any extra oil or fat.

Roasting is like a cozy nap in the oven. When you roast, you cook things in the oven until they turn golden and flavorful. It's like transforming plain veggies into crispy, flavorful bites that everyone loves.

Have you ever heard of blanching? It's like a quick dip in hot water followed by a cold bath. When you blanch, you cook ingredients in hot water for a short time, then you give them a chilly bath to keep their colors and flavors fresh.

And let's not forget about frying – it's like giving your ingredients a crispy makeover. When you fry, you cook ingredients in hot oil until they turn golden and deliciously crunchy. It's like making your own tasty treats!

Whether you're sautéing, baking, grilling, boiling, stir-frying, steaming, roasting, blanching, or frying, each technique adds a special touch to your cooking adventures. Just like a musician uses different notes to create beautiful melodies, you use different techniques to create mouthwatering dishes that make everyone's taste buds dance.

So, grab your apron and get ready to master these magical cooking techniques. With each flip of the pan and each turn of the oven knob, you're becoming a culinary superstar who can create incredible flavors and culinary wonders. Your kitchen is your stage, and these techniques are your tools – now let's cook up some delicious magic together!

CHAPTER 3

COOKING FOR EVERY OCCASION

CHAPTER 3 - COOKING FOR EVERY OCCASION

'WEEKNIGHT WONDERS: QUICK AND EASY RECIPES FOR BUSY YOUNG CHEFS'

Life can be a whirlwind of adventure and fun, and sometimes you need meals that match your energy. That's where weeknight wonders come to the rescue – delicious recipes that are quick, easy, and perfect for young chefs on the go. No matter how busy your day is, these recipes are like your culinary sidekicks, helping you create tasty dishes in no time.

Picture this: you've had an awesome day filled with laughter, learning, and play. Now, it's time for dinner, and you want something yummy, fast! That's where these weeknight wonders shine. They're like your trusty capes, swooping in to save the day and make sure you enjoy a fantastic meal.

Imagine cooking up a batch of super speedy stir-fry. You chop colorful veggies, toss them in a hot pan with a splash of sauce, and within minutes, you have a delicious dish that's bursting with flavor. It's like a quick adventure in the kitchen that ends with a tasty victory!

Or how about whipping up a delightful pasta dish? You boil pasta until it's tender, toss it with a yummy sauce, and voila – dinner is served! It's like creating a plate of comfort that's ready before you know it.

And let's not forget about making a scrumptious sandwich. You pile your favorite fillings between slices of bread, and in no time, you have a handheld feast that's both satisfying and tasty. It's like creating a mini masterpiece that fits right in your hands.

The magic of weeknight wonders is that they're like cooking superheroes – they save time without sacrificing flavor. They're perfect for those days when you want to enjoy a delicious meal without spending too much time in the kitchen.

Imagine you're a young chef with a busy schedule – school, activities, and fun adventures fill up your day. Weeknight wonders are like your culinary secret weapon, helping you create meals that are as exciting as your day.

With just a few ingredients and a dash of creativity, you can whip up meals that make you proud and your taste buds dance. And the best part? You're in charge! You can add your own twist, mix in your favorite flavors, and make these recipes uniquely yours.

Weeknight wonders are your passport to flavorful and fabulous dinners that fit right into your busy life. They're like a friendly hug from the kitchen, welcoming you after a day of adventures. With every stir of the spoon and every flip of the pan, you're becoming a young chef who can create culinary magic, even on the busiest of days.

The next time you're in a hurry but still want a delicious meal, turn to your trusty weeknight wonders. They're like your culinary best friends, ready to help you create tasty dishes that fuel your energy and fill your heart with happiness. From stir-fries to pasta dishes to sandwiches, these recipes are your secret to weeknight success. Let's get cooking and make every meal a delightful adventure!

'FAMILY FEASTS: CREATING MEMORABLE MEALS FOR LOVED ONES'

Family feasts are like special celebrations, where you get to create amazing meals that bring joy and happiness to your loved ones. Whether it's a weekend brunch or a holiday dinner, these recipes are your secret to making unforgettable memories.

Think of family feasts as a grand adventure in the kitchen. Just like a captain navigating a ship, you're in charge of crafting a meal that makes everyone's taste buds dance with delight. And guess what? You're not just making food – you're creating moments that will be cherished forever.

Imagine the sound of laughter echoing in the kitchen as you cook up a hearty stew. You chop vegetables, add flavorful ingredients, and let everything simmer to perfection. It's like a symphony of flavors that warms both tummies and hearts.

Or picture the excitement as you serve up a beautifully roasted chicken. You baste it with savory herbs, let it turn golden in the oven, and watch as everyone's eyes light up with anticipation. It's like a masterpiece that's as delightful to look at as it is to eat.

And let's not forget about desserts that bring smiles to every face. You might create a gooey chocolate cake that's the star of the dessert table or bake cookies that vanish in the blink of an eye. It's like adding a touch of sweetness to the already magical feast.

Family feasts aren't just about the food – they're about love, connection, and sharing joy with those you care about. When you cook for your family, you're giving them a gift straight from your heart. And when you gather around the table to enjoy the meal together, you're creating memories that last a lifetime.

Their smiles and "yum" sounds are like applause for your culinary talents. It's like your very own standing ovation, a celebration of the chef in you!

Creating family feasts is like weaving a tapestry of love and flavors. Every ingredient you choose, every dish you create, is like a thread that contributes to the masterpiece. And just like an artist adds colors to a canvas, you add flavors to your family's lives.

They're about bringing your loved ones together, sharing stories and laughter, and creating bonds that grow stronger with every delicious bite.

With every recipe you master, you're becoming a young chef who can create not only amazing dishes but also unforgettable moments. Family feasts are your chance to shine, to show your loved ones how much you care, and to share your culinary magic with the world.

Put on your apron, gather your ingredients, and get ready to create family feasts that warm hearts and fill bellies. Whether it's a holiday, a birthday, or just a regular day, every meal you make is a chance to show your love and creativity. Let's cook up joy, laughter, and delicious memories together!

'CELEBRATE WITH FLAIR: SHOWSTOPPING DISHES FOR SPECIAL OCCASIONS'

Visualize your kitchen as a stage, and you're the director of a grand culinary show. Celebrate with flair is like your chance to put on a dazzling performance, creating showstopping dishes that steal the spotlight at special occasions. From birthdays to holidays, these recipes are your secret to wowing everyone with your culinary magic.

Think of celebrate with flair as your chance to be a culinary artist. Just like a painter adds vibrant colors to a canvas, you add incredible flavors to your dishes. And when you present your creations, it's like unveiling a masterpiece that leaves everyone in awe.

You layer cake, frosting, and decorations to create a dessert masterpiece that's fit for a royal celebration. It's like turning a simple dessert into a work of art!

You arrange colorful fruits on a buttery crust, creating a dessert that's a feast for both the eyes and the taste buds. It's like capturing the essence of summer in every bite.

And let's not forget about savory showstoppers, like a golden roast that's fit for a feast. You season meat with aromatic herbs, roast it to perfection, and present it like a king's banquet. It's like creating a meal that's fit for royalty!

Celebrate with flair is all about turning ordinary ingredients into extraordinary creations. Just like a magician adds surprises to their act, you add unexpected twists to your recipes. Whether it's a sprinkle of edible glitter or a drizzle of colorful sauce, your creativity knows no bounds.

Think about the excitement in the room as you present your showstopping dishes to your family and friends. Their eyes widen, their smiles grow, and their taste buds dance with joy. It's like a standing ovation for your culinary talents!

Creating showstopping dishes is like sharing your love and creativity with the world. When you present a spectacular dessert or a jaw-dropping main course, you're telling a story through your food. And just like a storyteller captivates their audience, you captivate taste buds and hearts.

It's like your culinary red carpet moment, where you get to showcase your talents and create memories that will be cherished forever.

With every recipe you master, you're becoming a young chef who can turn simple ingredients into dazzling dishes. Celebrate with flair is your opportunity to create moments that bring joy, laughter, and deliciousness to those you care about.

From elegant desserts to showstopping mains, every dish you make is like a performance that leaves everyone applauding. Let's celebrate with flair and make every occasion unforgettable!

CHAPTER 4

NAVIGATING CULINARY ADVENTURES

CHAPTER 4 - NAVIGATING CULINARY ADVENTURES

'EXPLORING GLOBAL FLAVORS: EMBARKING ON A JOURNEY THROUGH INTERNATIONAL CUISINE'

Close your eyes and imagine you're on a magical journey around the world. Each country you visit is like a treasure trove of flavors waiting to be discovered. Exploring global flavors is like your passport to a culinary adventure, where you get to taste the world's most delicious dishes right in your kitchen.

Think of global flavors as your chance to be a culinary explorer. Just like a detective following clues, you're uncovering the secrets of different cuisines and adding a touch of magic to your dishes. And guess what? Your taste buds are the ultimate adventurers, ready to savor new and exciting flavors.

Imagine cooking up a batch of flavorful tacos that transport you to the streets of Mexico. You fill soft tortillas with seasoned meat, fresh veggies, and zesty salsa. It's like a fiesta in your mouth that's bursting with colors and flavors.

You mix aromatic spices, tender meat, and creamy sauce, creating a dish that's a masterpiece of flavor. It's like a journey to a faraway land with every delicious bite.

Let's not forget about sushi that brings the tastes of Japan to your plate. You roll rice, veggies, and seafood into delicate bites, creating a dish that's as beautiful as it is delicious. It's like a taste of the ocean and a culinary adventure in one!

Exploring global flavors is all about expanding your culinary horizons. Just like an explorer discovers new lands, you're discovering new tastes that make your dishes unforgettable. Whether it's a sprinkle of exotic spices or a drizzle of tangy sauce, your creativity knows no bounds.

Immerse yourself in the role of chef and serve dishes from all backgrounds to your family and friends. Their taste buds embark on their own journey and their eyes light up with joy. It's like bringing the flavors of the world into your own kitchen!

Creating dishes from around the globe is like sharing a piece of culture and tradition with your loved ones. When you cook a dish from a different country, you're not just making food – you're telling a story and paying homage to the people who created the recipe.

That exploring global flavors is like setting sail on a delicious journey. It's like bringing the world's most exciting tastes to your very own kitchen, turning every meal into an epic experience.

With every recipe you master, you're becoming a young chef who can create dishes that span across continents. Exploring global flavors is your opportunity to broaden your culinary knowledge, impress your taste buds, and share your love for food with those you care about.

Get ready to embark on a journey through international cuisine. From tacos to curries to sushi, every dish you make is like a ticket to a different part of the world. Let's explore global flavors and make every meal an exciting adventure for your taste buds!

'CREATIVE FUSION: BLENDING TRADITIONS AND INNOVATIONS IN MODERN COOKING'

Creative fusion is like your laboratory of deliciousness, where you get to blend traditions and innovations to create dishes that are both unique and tasty. It's like cooking up a storm of exciting ideas in your very own kitchen!

Just like an artist combines colors to create amazing paintings, you combine ingredients to make dishes that are a feast for the eyes and the taste buds. And guess what? Your kitchen is your playground of possibilities, where you can experiment and create new flavors.

Create a dish that's a fusion of two cultures, like a taco pizza that brings together the best of Mexico and Italy. You top a pizza crust with taco-inspired ingredients like seasoned meat and vibrant veggies. It's like a delicious experiment that results in a taste explosion!

Or try to making sushi burritos that combine the flavors of Japan and Mexico. You wrap sushi ingredients in a tortilla, creating a handheld masterpiece that's both familiar and excitingly new. It's like a culinary adventure you can hold in your hand!

And let's not forget about desserts that fuse sweet and savory, like bacon-studded chocolate chip cookies. You add bits of crispy bacon to a classic cookie dough, creating a treat that's unexpected and totally delicious. It's like a flavor party in your mouth!

Creative fusion is all about thinking outside the box and trying new things. Just like an explorer discovers uncharted lands, you're discovering uncharted flavors that make your dishes unforgettable. Whether it's a sprinkle of unexpected spices or a surprising combination of ingredients, your creativity knows no bounds.

Imagine the wonder on your family and friends' faces as they try your creative fusion dishes. Their eyes widen, their taste buds dance, and they can't help but be amazed by the unique and exciting flavors you've created. It's like serving up a plate of pure excitement!

Creating dishes that blend traditions and innovations is like showing that there are no limits to your creativity. When you take inspiration from different cuisines and add your own twist, you're creating dishes that are uniquely yours and telling your own culinary story.

With every recipe you master, you're becoming a young chef who can think beyond the ordinary. Creative fusion is your chance to play with flavors, experiment with ingredients, and create dishes that showcase your culinary ingenuity.

Put on your chef's hat, gather your ingredients, and get ready to mix, match, and innovate in the kitchen. From taco pizzas to sushi burritos to bacon cookies, every dish you make is like a masterpiece that's both delicious and exciting. Let's get creative and make every meal a one-of-a-kind culinary adventure!

CHAPTER 5

HEALTHFUL AND WHOLESOME COOKING

CHAPTER 5: HEALTHFUL AND WHOLESOME COOKING

'FROM FARM TO TABLE: EMBRACING FRESH, SEASONAL INGREDIENTS'

Imagine stepping into a magical garden where the air is filled with the scents of ripe fruits and colorful vegetables. From farm to table is like your journey to discover the freshest and tastiest ingredients that nature has to offer. It's like bringing the flavors of the earth straight to your plate, creating dishes that burst with goodness!

Think of from farm to table as your chance to be a nature explorer. Just like a detective searching for hidden treasures, you're on a mission to find the most delicious ingredients that grow in the ground and on trees. And guess what? Your taste buds are the ultimate detectives, ready to savor the goodness of nature.

Slice, add the salad and a pinch of spicy, to create an explosion of extraordinary flavor.

You blend the berries into a sweet sauce, pour it over ice cream, and take a spoonful of pure deliciousness. It's like tasting the sweetness of summer in every bite.

You might roast colorful bell peppers until they're tender and sweet or sauté vibrant greens until they're perfectly crisp. It's like turning nature's bounty into dishes that make your heart and taste buds happy.

From farm to table is all about celebrating the goodness of nature. Just like a gardener tends to plants, you're tending to your dishes, making sure they're filled with the freshest and tastiest ingredients. Whether it's a sprinkle of herbs or a handful of berries, your dishes are like a tribute to the earth's bounty.

The satisfaction as you serve up dishes made with ingredients that you've picked yourself or chosen from the farmer's market. The colors are brighter, the flavors are richer, and you can't help but feel a deep connection to the earth. It's like a celebration of nature's gifts!

Creating dishes with fresh, seasonal ingredients is like showing love and respect for the planet. When you choose ingredients that are in season, you're not only enjoying the best flavors but also supporting local farmers and the environment.

Remember that from farm to table is like a journey of flavors straight from the earth. It's like turning your kitchen into a haven of freshness and creating dishes that are not only delicious but also good for you and the planet.

With every recipe you master, you're becoming a young chef who understands the beauty of nature's bounty. From fruits to veggies to herbs, from farm to table is your opportunity to create dishes that showcase the goodness of the earth and celebrate the magic of fresh ingredients.

So get ready to embrace the deliciousness of nature's gifts. From garden-fresh salads to vibrant veggie dishes, every meal you make is like a tribute to the flavors of the earth. Let's celebrate the magic of from farm to table and make every dish a true taste of nature!

'NOURISHING CREATIONS: BALANCING TASTE AND NUTRITION IN EVERY BITE'

Nourishing creations are like your way of fueling your body with delicious dishes that are not only tasty but also good for you. It's like becoming a culinary scientist, creating meals that give you energy and keep you strong!

Think of nourishing creations as your chance to be a food wizard. Just like a magician combines elements to create magic, you combine ingredients to make dishes that are both yummy and nutritious. And guess what? Your body is your ultimate fan, ready to thrive with every nourishing bite.

Imagine making a colorful salad that's like a rainbow on your plate. You add crisp veggies, juicy fruits, and crunchy nuts, creating a dish that's a burst of flavors and nutrients. It's like turning a simple salad into a superhero meal!

You blend together fruits, yogurt, and a splash of milk, creating a drink that's like a burst of energy in a glass. It's like starting your day with a superhero boost!

You might create a plate with lean protein, whole grains, and lots of colorful veggies. It's like giving your body everything it needs to feel strong and vibrant.

Nourishing creations are all about finding the perfect balance between taste and nutrition. Just like an athlete needs the right gear to perform, you need the right food to power your adventures. Whether it's a sprinkle of seeds or a drizzle of healthy fats, your dishes are like a superhero costume for your body!

Imagine the satisfaction of knowing that you're giving your body the best fuel it needs to stay active and healthy. As you savor each bite, you're not just enjoying the flavors – you're nourishing your body and giving it the energy to conquer the day.

Creating dishes that balance taste and nutrition is like showing love and care for yourself. When you choose ingredients that are good for you, you're not only enjoying delicious meals but also taking care of your body like the superhero it is.

That nourishing creations are like your way of giving your body the power it needs. It's like becoming a culinary hero, creating dishes that make your taste buds sing and your body feel strong.

With every recipe you master, you're becoming a young chef who understands the importance of eating well. Nourishing creations are your chance to create meals that are both delicious and beneficial, turning every bite into a step towards a healthier and happier you.

Do not wait any longer, roll up your sleeves and give the best of yourself! From colorful salads to energetic shakes to balanced meals, every dish you make is like a little gift to yourself - a delicious reminder that you're feeding your body the best way possible!

CHAPTER 6
THE ART
OF BAKING

CHAPTER 6 - THE ART OF BAKING

'SWEET SENSATIONS: MASTERING THE BASICS OF BAKING FOR YOUNG PASTRY CHEFS'

Imagine your kitchen as a magical bakery, where the air is filled with the scent of warm cookies and freshly baked cakes. Sweet sensations are like your journey into the world of baking, where you get to create mouthwatering treats that make everyone's taste buds dance with delight. It's like becoming a pastry wizard, conjuring up desserts that are as tasty as they are beautiful!

Think of sweet sensations as your chance to be a dessert artist. Just like a painter uses brushes to create art, you use ingredients to create edible masterpieces. And guess what? Your kitchen is your canvas, ready to be filled with the colors and flavors of your imagination.

Imagine mixing up a batch of cookie dough that's so tempting, you can hardly resist taking a taste. You scoop spoonfuls onto a baking sheet and watch as the dough turns into perfectly golden cookies. It's like creating edible happiness that fills your home with sweet aromas.

You stack layers of moist cake and creamy frosting, creating a dessert that's like a work of art. It's like turning flour and sugar into a sweet masterpiece!

You swirl frosting onto each cupcake and add colorful sprinkles, creating treats that are as fun to make as they are to eat. It's like a party in every bite!

Sweet sensations are all about mastering the art of baking. Just like a musician practices their instrument, you practice your skills to create desserts that are a feast for the eyes and the taste buds. Whether it's a sprinkle of sugar or a drizzle of chocolate, your creations are like little moments of sweetness!

Imagine the pride you feel as you serve up your baked treats to your family and friends. Their eyes light up, their smiles grow wide, and they can't wait to dive into the deliciousness you've made. Imagine as if an amusement park suddenly became your kitchen!

Cooking sweets for loved ones is an indescribable satisfaction, it means giving a part of yourself to the one who goes to enjoy the delicious dish. And every bite they take is like a taste of your love and creativity.

That sweet sensations are like your way of spreading joy through delicious treats. It's like turning your kitchen into a bakery where every dessert is made with love and magic.

With every recipe you master, you're becoming a young pastry chef who can create desserts that bring smiles and happiness. Sweet sensations are your opportunity to learn the art of baking, turning flour and sugar into delightful creations that make the world a sweeter place.

Get start to create desserts that are as beautiful as they are tasty. From cookies to cakes to cupcakes, every treat you make is like a little slice of sweetness that brings joy to everyone's day. Let's bake up some sweet sensations and make every bite a delightful adventure!

'BAKING BEYOND THE BASICS: ELEVATING YOUR DESSERTS TO THE NEXT LEVEL'

Baking beyond the basics is like your ticket to a world of dessert magic, where you get to take your sweet creations to new heights and dazzle everyone's taste buds. It's like becoming a dessert genius, crafting treats that are as imaginative as they are delicious!

Baking beyond the basics as your chance to be a dessert innovator. Just like an inventor comes up with new ideas, you come up with exciting twists that make your desserts stand out. And guess what? Your kitchen is your laboratory, where you mix and match flavors to create edible wonders.

Turning a simple chocolate cake into a masterpiece that's filled with surprises. You might add layers of creamy filling, drizzle on caramel sauce, and top it all off with a sprinkle of crushed nuts. It's like creating a dessert that's as exciting to look at as it is to eat!

Add a pinch of spices or mix in colorful candies, creating treats that are like little treasures waiting to be discovered. It's like a flavor adventure in every bite!

You might swirl on frosting in vibrant colors, add edible glitter for extra sparkle, and create designs that are almost too beautiful to eat. It's like turning each cupcake into a tiny masterpiece!

Baking beyond the basics is all about pushing your creativity to the limits. Just like an artist experiments with colors, you experiment with flavors and techniques to create desserts that are uniquely yours. Whether it's a swirl of frosting or a sprinkle of edible decorations, your desserts are like a canvas waiting for your imagination to come to life.

Think about the sense of accomplishment as you present your inventive desserts to your family and friends. Their eyes widen, their taste buds are in for a surprise, and they can't help but be amazed by the imaginative treats you've created. It's like serving up a plate of pure delight!

Creating desserts that go beyond the basics is like showing that you're not afraid to take risks and try new things. When you put your own twist on classic recipes, you're not just making desserts – you're making memories and sharing your love for baking with others.

With every recipe you master, you're becoming a young baking artist who knows how to turn ordinary ingredients into extraordinary desserts. Baking beyond the basics is your opportunity to let your creativity shine, turning each treat into a masterpiece that's uniquely yours.

Get ready to take your desserts to the next level. From cakes to cookies to cupcakes, every creation you make is like a piece of art that's as fun to make as it is to enjoy. Let's bake beyond the basics and make every dessert a masterpiece of flavor and imagination!

CHAPTER 7

KITCHEN CONFIDENCE AND BEYOND

CHAPTER 7 - KITCHEN CONFIDENCE AND BEYOND

'OVERCOMING KITCHEN DISASTERS: TURNING MISTAKES INTO LEARNING OPPORTUNITIES'

Overcoming kitchen disasters is like your secret potion for transforming mishaps into moments of learning and growth. It's like becoming a kitchen detective, solving culinary mysteries and turning oops into aha!

Think of overcoming kitchen disasters as your chance to be a culinary hero. Just like a problem solver cracks codes, you crack the code to fixing cooking mishaps. And guess what? Your kitchen is your playground, where you can experiment, learn, and turn any situation around.

Imagine the time you accidentally added too much salt to a dish and turned it into a taste sensation. You might balance out the flavors with a pinch of sugar or add more ingredients to dilute the salty taste. It's like turning a mistake into a culinary victory!

And be careful to set the timer correctly. You could scrape away the burnt bits, sandwich the cookies with a layer of frosting, and create biscuit sandwiches that are even more delicious than you would expect. It's like magic in the kitchen!

Overcoming kitchen disasters is all about embracing challenges and finding creative solutions. Just like an explorer faces obstacles and keeps going, you face cooking challenges and turn them into opportunities to learn and improve. Whether it's a dash of creativity or a sprinkle of ingenuity, your kitchen is your stage for culinary success stories.

As you transform mistakes into delicious discoveries, you're not just saving a dish – you're gaining valuable skills and becoming a more confident young chef. It's like adding a sprinkle of confidence to every meal!

Overcoming kitchen disasters is like showing that you're not afraid to tackle challenges head-on. When you approach mistakes as chances to learn and grow, you're not just cooking – you're building resilience and a can-do attitude that will serve you well in the kitchen and beyond.

So, the next time you encounter a kitchen mishap, remember that overcoming disasters is like your superpower. It's like turning your kitchen into a classroom where every mistake is a lesson waiting to be learned. With a little creativity and a dash of determination, you can turn any kitchen oops into a tasty triumph!

With every cooking adventure you embark on, you're becoming a young chef who knows that mistakes are just stepping stones to success. Overcoming kitchen disasters is your opportunity to build skills, confidence, and a positive attitude that will make you shine in the kitchen and in life.

Let's turn kitchen disasters into delicious learning opportunities and make every cooking adventure a chance to shine!

'SHARING THE LOVE: COOKING FOR FRIENDS, FAMILY, AND BEYOND'

Imagine your kitchen as a stage where you become the star of your very own cooking show. In the chapter titled "Sharing the Love: Cooking for Friends, Family, and Beyond," you'll learn how to spread joy and deliciousness with every dish you create. It's like becoming a culinary superhero, using your skills to make the world a tastier and happier place.

Cooking with Love

Think of your kitchen as a place where you can sprinkle love into every recipe. Whether you're whipping up a batch of cookies or crafting a family dinner, your love and passion for cooking shine through in every bite. It's like a secret ingredient that makes your dishes extra special and memorable.

Family Feasts and Friend Gatherings

Imagine the excitement of preparing a feast for your loved ones. From family dinners to gatherings with friends, your cooking has the power to bring people together and create lasting memories. Just like a conductor leads an orchestra, you'll orchestrate a meal that's not just delicious but also filled with laughter and connection.

Spreading Happiness Beyond Your Kitchen

Cooking for friends, family, and beyond is like sharing your happiness on a plate. Whether you're baking cookies for a school event or preparing a surprise meal for a neighbor, your cooking becomes a gift that brings smiles to faces and warms hearts. It's like creating happiness that's meant to be shared.

Becoming a Culinary Ambassador

Sharing your love for cooking is like becoming a culinary ambassador. As you serve up dishes that reflect your creativity and care, you're showing the world the magic that happens in your kitchen. Your cooking becomes a way to express yourself and bring a touch of your personality to every meal.

Creating Lasting Memories

Imagine the joy on your family's faces as they taste the delicious meals you've prepared. Every dish you make becomes a memory that you'll cherish forever. Whether it's a holiday feast or a simple Sunday brunch, your cooking has the power to create moments that become part of your family's story.

Spreading Kindness Through Cooking

Cooking for friends, family, and beyond is like a sprinkle of kindness in the world. When you share your culinary creations, you're not just feeding hungry stomachs – you're feeding hearts and souls. It's like sending a message of love and care through every bite.

Your Culinary Legacy

Imagine the impact you can make by cooking for others. Your delicious creations become part of your culinary legacy, something that people will remember and talk about for years to come. Whether you're baking cookies for a school event or making dinner for your family, your cooking leaves a positive mark on the world.

So, the next time you're in the kitchen, remember that cooking for friends, family, and beyond is like a gift you give to the world. It's like a way of showing your love, creativity, and kindness through the dishes you create. With each meal you make, you're spreading happiness and making the world a tastier place for everyone.

As you cook for your loved ones and share your culinary talents, you're creating connections and leaving a delicious legacy. Just like a storyteller shares tales, you're sharing your love for cooking and creating a story that's as heartwarming as it is delicious. So, put on your apron, gather your ingredients, and let the joy of cooking for others be your secret recipe for making the world a better and yummier place!

CHAPTER 8

BREAKFAST

RECIPES

MAGICAL UNICORN SMOOTHIE BOWL

Preparation Time: 10 minutes - Ingredients:

- 1 cup frozen mixed berries (blueberries, strawberries, raspberries)
- 1 ripe banana
- 1/2 cup Greek yogurt
- 1/2 cup almond milk (or any milk of your taste)
- 1 tablespoon honey or maple syrup (optional)
- Toppings: sliced kiwi, fresh berries, granola, chia seeds, edible glitter (optional)

Procedure:

- Put the berries, yoghurt and the banana and almonds in a blender.
- Blend the ingredients until you have a smooth and creamy consistency.
- If you'd like a touch of sweetness, you can add honey or maple syrup and blend again.
- Pour the smoothie mixture into a bowl.
- Now comes the fun part! Create swirls of different colors in the smoothie bowl using the back of a spoon. Imagine you're painting a rainbow in your bowl!
- Arrange the sliced kiwi, fresh berries, and granola in rows on top of the colorful swirls.
- Sprinkle chia seeds for a little crunch and extra nutrition.
- If you're feeling extra magical, add a pinch of edible glitter to make your smoothie bowl sparkle like a unicorn!
- Enjoy your enchanting creation with a spoon and savor the vibrant flavors and textures.

FLUFFY CLOUD PANCAKES WITH BERRY DRIZZLE

Preparation Time: 20 minutes - Ingredients:

- 1 cup all-purpose flour
- 2 tablespoons sugar
- 1 teaspoon baking powder
- 1/2 teaspoon baking soda
- 1/4 teaspoon salt
- 3/4 cup buttermilk
- 1/4 cup milk
- 1 egg
- 2 tablespoons melted butter
- 1 teaspoon vanilla extract
- Cooking spray or butter for the pan
- Fresh berries for garnish (blueberries, strawberries, raspberries)
- Maple syrup or honey

Procedure:

- Mix in a flour, baking powder and baking soda bowl and add a pinch of salt.
- In a separate bowl, whisk together the buttermilk, milk, egg, melted butter, and vanilla extract until well combined.
- Enter all the ingredients and mix until you get a mixture, it's okay even if there is some lumps.
- Place in a non-stick pan preheated cooking spray or a knob of butter.
- Pour about 1/4 cup of the pancake batter onto the skillet for each pancake.
- Cook until you see bubbles forming on the surface and the edges look slightly set for 2-3 minutes.
- Carefully flip the pancakes with a spatula and cook for an additional 2-3 minutes, or until they are golden brown on both sides and cooked through.
- While the pancakes are cooking, you can prepare the berry drizzle. In a blender, puree a handful of fresh berries until smooth. If you want, you can strain the puree to remove any seeds.

- Once the pancakes are ready, stack them on a plate and drizzle the berry puree over the top.
- Garnish with additional fresh berries for an extra burst of flavor and color.
- Serve the fluffy cloud pancakes with a drizzle of maple syrup or honey on the side.
- Enjoy your stack of fluffy goodness and savor the delightful combination of fluffy pancakes and tangy berry drizzle!

MINI BREAKFAST BURRITO BITES

Preparation Time: 15 minutes - Ingredients:

- 4 small flour tortillas (6-inch diameter)
- 4 large eggs
- 1/4 cup diced bell peppers (any color)
- 1/4 cup diced onions
- 1/4 cup shredded cheddar cheese
- 2 tablespoons chopped fresh cilantro
- Salt and pepper to taste
- Cooking spray or oil

Procedure:

- In a bowl, beat the eggs and season with a pinch of salt and pepper.
- Heat a non-stick skillet over medium heat and lightly grease it with cooking spray or a small amount of oil.
- Add the diced bell peppers and onions to the skillet and sauté until they're slightly softened and aromatic.
- Pour the beaten eggs into the skillet with the sautéed vegetables.
- Gently scramble the eggs until they're cooked through and no longer runny. Remove from heat.
- Place the tortillas in a preheated pan until soft.
- Lay out each tortilla and place a spoonful of the scrambled eggs in the center.
- Sprinkle shredded cheddar cheese and chopped cilantro on top of the eggs.
- Once the filling is in, fold the tortilla and make a burrito.
- Place the mini breakfast burritos seam side down on a serving platter.
- If desired, you can secure the burritos with toothpicks to keep them from unwrapping.
- Serve the mini breakfast burrito bites with a side of salsa, sour cream, or guacamole for dipping.
- Enjoy these flavorful and compact breakfast bites that are perfect for munching on the go!

PEANUT BUTTER BANANA ROLL-UPS

Preparation Time: 10 minutes - Ingredients:

- 2 whole wheat tortillas
- 2 ripe bananas
- 4 tablespoons peanut butter
- 2 tablespoons honey
- 1/4 teaspoon ground cinnamon (optional)
- Chopped nuts (such as almonds or walnuts) for garnish (optional)

Procedure:

- Lay out the whole wheat tortillas on a clean surface.
- Spread 2 tablespoons of peanut butter evenly over each tortilla, leaving a small border around the edges.
- Spread 1 tablespoon of honey over the peanut butter tortillas.
- If using ground cinnamon, sprinkle a pinch over the honey.
- Peel the ripe bananas and place one banana on the lower third of each tortilla.
- Gently roll up the tortilla, tucking in the sides as you go, to create a snug wrap around the banana.
- If desired, you can secure the roll-ups with toothpicks to keep them in place.
- Using a sharp knife, carefully slice each rolled tortilla into bite-sized pieces.
- Arrange the peanut butter banana roll-ups on a plate.
- If using chopped nuts, sprinkle them over the top of the roll-ups for an extra crunch and nutty flavor.
- Serve these delicious roll-ups as a nutritious and satisfying breakfast or snack.
- Enjoy the perfect combination of creamy peanut butter, sweet banana, and a hint of honey in every bite!

CHOCOLATE CHIP OATMEAL PANCAKE STACK

Preparation Time: 20 minutes - Ingredients:

- 1 cup rolled oats
- 1 cup milk (any type)
- 1 large egg
- 1 tablespoon melted butter
- 2 tablespoons brown sugar
- 1 teaspoon vanilla extract
- 1/2 cup all-purpose flour
- 1 teaspoon baking powder
- 1/4 teaspoon salt
- 1/4 cup mini chocolate chips
- Cooking spray or butter for the pan
- Maple syrup and additional chocolate chips for serving

Procedure:

- In a blender, combine the rolled oats and milk. Let it sit for about 5 minutes to soften the oats.
- Add the egg, melted butter, brown sugar, and vanilla extract to the oat mixture. Blend until smooth.
- In a mixing bowl, whisk together the all-purpose flour, baking powder, and salt.
- Pour the oat mixture into the bowl with the dry ingredients and gently stir until just combined.
- Fold in the mini chocolate chips into the batter.
- Place cooking spray or butter on a preheated non-stick pan.
- Pour about 1/4 cup of the pancake batter onto the skillet for each pancake.
- Cook until bubbles form on the surface and the edges look set for 2-3 minutes.
- Carefully flip the pancakes with a spatula and cook for an additional 2-3 minutes, or until they are golden brown on both sides and cooked through.
- Stack the chocolate chip oatmeal pancakes on a plate as you cook.

- Drizzle maple syrup over the top of the stack and sprinkle some additional mini chocolate chips for extra chocolatey goodness.
- Serve the pancake stack with a fork and indulge in the delightful combination of fluffy pancakes and melty chocolate chips.

CHAPTER 9

LUNCH

RECIPES

OUT-OF-THIS-WORLD RAINBOW SALAD JAR

Preparation Time: 15 minutes - Ingredients:

- 1 cup cooked quinoa or your favorite grain
- 1/2 cup diced bell peppers (red, orange, yellow)
- 1/2 cup diced cucumber
- 1/2 cup shredded carrots
- 1/4 cup diced red cabbage
- 1/4 cup cherry tomatoes, halved
- 1/4 cup crumbled feta cheese or your favorite cheese
- 2 tablespoons chopped fresh herbs (such as parsley or basil)
- 2 tablespoons balsamic vinaigrette or dressing of your choice
- Salt and pepper to taste

Procedure:

- Begin by layering the ingredients in a glass jar in the following order:
- Start with the balsamic vinaigrette or dressing at the bottom of the jar.
- Next, add the cooked quinoa or grain as the first layer.
- Layer the diced bell peppers, followed by the diced cucumber.
- Add the shredded carrots and diced red cabbage for a burst of color.
- Toss in the cherry tomato halves for a juicy touch.
- Sprinkle the crumbled feta cheese over the vegetables.
- Finish by adding the chopped fresh herbs for a burst of flavor.
- Seal the jar tightly with a lid and refrigerate until you're ready to enjoy your salad.
- When you're ready to eat, give the jar a good shake to mix all the flavors and dress the salad.
- Pour the colorful rainbow salad onto a plate or into a bowl.
- Season with a pinch of salt and pepper to taste.
- Toss the salad to ensure that all the ingredients are coated with the dressing.
- Enjoy a wholesome and vibrant lunch that's as visually appealing as it is delicious!

MINI VEGGIE PIZZA FACES

Preparation Time: 15 minutes - Ingredients:

- 4 whole wheat English muffins, split and toasted
- 1/2 cup tomato sauce or pizza sauce
- 1 cup shredded mozzarella cheese
- Assorted vegetable toppings: sliced bell peppers, cherry tomatoes, sliced black olives, sliced mushrooms, etc.
- Sliced cheese (such as cheddar or provolone) for creating faces
- Fresh basil leaves for garnish
- Olive oil
- Salt and pepper to taste

Procedure:

- Preheat the oven to 375°F (190°C).
- Lay out the toasted English muffin halves on a baking sheet.
- Spread a spoonful of tomato or pizza sauce over each muffin half.
- Sprinkle shredded mozzarella cheese over the sauce.
- Arrange the assorted vegetable toppings over the cheese to create colorful faces.
- For example, you can use sliced bell peppers for eyes, cherry tomatoes for noses, and sliced olives for mouths.
- Create faces by cutting shapes from sliced cheese, such as using a star shape for eyes or a half-circle for a smile.
- Drizzle a tiny amount of olive oil over the veggies and cheese for added flavor.
- Season with a pinch of salt and pepper to taste.
- Place the baking sheet in the preheated oven and bake for about 8-10 minutes, or until the cheese is melted and bubbly.
- Keep a close eye on the pizzas to avoid over-browning the toppings.
- Once the mini veggie pizza faces are ready, remove them from the oven and let them cool slightly.
- Garnish with fresh basil leaves for a burst of color and a touch of freshness.
- Serve these adorable mini veggie pizza faces for a fun and nutritious lunch that kids and adults will enjoy!

CRUNCHY CHICKEN TENDERS ADVENTURE

Preparation Time: 20 minutes - Ingredients:

- 1 pound boneless, skinless chicken tenders
- 1 cup panko breadcrumbs
- 1/2 cup grated Parmesan cheese
- 1 teaspoon garlic powder
- 1/2 teaspoon paprika
- Salt and pepper to taste
- 2 large eggs
- Cooking spray or oil for baking

Procedure:

- Preheat the oven to 400°F (200°C) and line a baking sheet with parchment paper.
- In a shallow dish, combine the panko breadcrumbs, grated Parmesan cheese, garlic powder, paprika, salt, and pepper. Mix well.
- Whisk the eggs until well beaten in a second dish.
- Put the chicken in the eggs.
- Then insert into the breadcrumbs.
- Place the coated chicken tender onto the prepared baking sheet.
- Repeat the process with the remaining chicken tenders.
- Lightly spray or brush the tops of the chicken tenders with cooking spray or a small amount of oil. This helps them achieve a crispy texture.
- Bake the chicken tenders in the preheated oven for about 15-18 minutes, or until they are golden brown and cooked through.
- Remember to turn the meat halfway through cooking for a uniform crispness.
- Once finished cooking let them cool.
- Serve on a plate with sauce to taste.
- Enjoy this unique crunch with whoever you want!

HOMEMADE MAC 'N' CHEESE DELIGHT

Preparation Time: 25 minutes - Ingredients:

- 8 ounces elbow macaroni or your favorite pasta
- 2 cups shredded sharp cheddar cheese
- 1/2 cup grated Parmesan cheese
- 3 cups milk (any type)
- 1/4 cup unsalted butter
- 1/4 cup all-purpose flour
- 1/2 teaspoon garlic powder
- 1/2 teaspoon onion powder
- Salt and pepper to taste
- Bread crumbs for topping (optional)

Procedure:

- Cook the pasta according to the instructions.
- Melt butter over medium heat.
- Stir in the all-purpose flour to create a smooth paste (roux). Cook for about 1-2 minutes, stirring constantly.
- Gradually whisk in the milk, making sure to break up any lumps.
- Beat over low heat until a thick consistency forms.
- Reduce the heat to low and stir in the shredded cheddar cheese and grated Parmesan cheese. Keep stirring until the cheeses are melted and the sauce is creamy.
- Season the cheese sauce with garlic powder, onion powder, salt, and pepper. Adjust the seasonings to taste.
- Add the cooked macaroni or pasta to the cheese sauce and stir to coat the pasta evenly with the creamy cheese mixture.
- If desired, you can preheat the oven to 375°F (190°C) and transfer the mac 'n' cheese to a baking dish.
- Sprinkle bread crumbs over the top for a crispy crust.
- Bake in the preheated oven for about 15-20 minutes, or until the top is golden and bubbly.
- If you're not baking, simply serve the homemade mac 'n' cheese directly from the stovetop.

- Spoon the mac 'n' cheese into bowls and savor every creamy and cheesy bite.

COLORFUL RAINBOW WRAPS WITH HUMMUS

Preparation Time: 15 minutes - Ingredients:

- Large whole wheat or spinach tortilla wraps
- 1 cup hummus (store-bought or homemade)
- Assorted colorful vegetables for filling: sliced bell peppers (red, orange, yellow), shredded carrots, cucumber slices, baby spinach leaves, grated beets, etc.
- Optional: sliced avocado for creaminess
- Salt and pepper to taste

Procedure:

- Lay out the tortilla wrap on a clean surface.
- Spreading hummus all over the surface.
- Arrange the assorted colorful vegetables over one half of the wrap, leaving a border around the edges.
- If using avocado, place slices over the veggies.
- Season the vegetables with a pinch of salt and pepper to taste.
- Gently fold the side of the wrap without vegetables over the vegetable-filled side.
- Begin rolling the wrap from the filled side, tucking in the edges as you go.
- Roll tightly to create a neat and compact wrap.
- Slice the wrap in half diagonally to reveal the colorful layers inside.
- If desired, secure each half with toothpicks for easy handling.
- Serve these vibrant and delicious rainbow wraps with a side of extra hummus for dipping.

CHAPTER 10
DINNER
RECIPES

STARRY NIGHT SPAGHETTI AND VEGGIE MEATBALLS

Preparation Time: 35 minutes - Ingredients:

- 8 ounces whole wheat spaghetti
  - For Veggie Meatballs:
  - 1 cup cooked and mashed chickpeas
  - 1/2 cup breadcrumbs
  - 1/4 cup grated Parmesan cheese
  - 1/4 cup finely chopped onion
  - 1/4 cup finely chopped bell peppers
  - 1 garlic clove, minced
  - 1 teaspoon dried oregano
  - Salt and pepper to taste
  - Olive oil for cooking
  - For Tomato Sauce:
  - 2 cups tomato sauce (store-bought or homemade)
  - 1 teaspoon dried basil
  - 1 teaspoon dried oregano
- Fresh basil leaves for garnish (optional)

Procedure:

- Cook the whole wheat spaghetti according to the package instructions. Drain and set aside.
- In a mixing bowl, combine the mashed chickpeas, breadcrumbs, grated Parmesan cheese, chopped onion, chopped bell peppers, minced garlic, dried oregano, salt, and pepper. Mix until well combined.
- Form with the mixture of small meatballs.
- In a skillet, heat a drizzle of olive oil over medium heat.
- Add the veggie meatballs to the skillet and cook until they are golden brown on all sides and cooked through, about 10-12 minutes.
- In another saucepan, heat the tomato sauce over medium heat.
- Add basil and oregani and let simmer for a few minutes.
- Gently add the cooked veggie meatballs to the tomato sauce, allowing them to soak up the flavors.
- Serve the veggie meatballs and tomato sauce over a portion of cooked whole wheat spaghetti.

- Garnish with fresh basil leaves for an extra burst of flavor and color.
- Enjoy the Starry Night Spaghetti and Veggie Meatballs with a side of your favorite steamed vegetables or a simple green salad.

FIESTA BURRITO BOWL WITH ZESTY GUACAMOLE

Preparation Time: 30 minutes - Ingredients:

- 1 cup cooked brown rice or quinoa
- 1 cup black beans, drained and rinsed
- 1 cup cooked corn kernels (fresh, frozen, or canned)
- 1 cup diced bell peppers (assorted colors)
- 1 cup diced tomatoes
- 1 cup chopped lettuce or mixed greens
- 1/2 cup diced red onion
- 1/4 cup chopped fresh cilantro
- 1 cup cooked and seasoned ground turkey (optional)
  - For Zesty Guacamole:
  - 2 ripe avocados, peeled and pitted
  - 1/4 cup diced red onion
  - Juice of 1 lime
  - 1 small garlic clove, minced
  - 1/4 teaspoon cumin
  - Salt and pepper to taste

Procedure:

- Prepare the brown rice or quinoa according to the package instructions. Fluff with a fork and set aside.
- In a mixing bowl, combine the black beans, cooked corn kernels, diced bell peppers, diced tomatoes, chopped lettuce or mixed greens, diced red onion, and chopped cilantro.
- If using, add the seasoned ground turkey to the bowl.
- Toss the ingredients together to create a colorful and flavorful burrito bowl mixture.
- In a separate bowl, mash the avocados and create the guacamole base.
- Add the diced red onion, lime juice, minced garlic, cumin, salt, and pepper to the mashed avocados. Mix well to combine.
- Assemble the Fiesta Burrito Bowl by layering a portion of the cooked brown rice or quinoa at the bottom of a bowl.
- Top with the colorful burrito bowl mixture, arranging it in sections.
- Spoon a generous dollop of zesty guacamole onto the bowl.

- Garnish with extra chopped cilantro if desired.
- Serve the Fiesta Burrito Bowl with Zesty Guacamole and enjoy a fiesta of flavors and textures in every bite!

MAGICAL GARDEN VEGGIE STIR-FRY

Preparation Time: 20 minutes - Ingredients:

- 2 cups mixed vegetables (broccoli florets, bell peppers, snap peas, carrots, etc.), sliced
- 1 cup firm tofu or tempeh, cubed (optional)
- 1 tablespoon sesame oil or vegetable oil
- 2 tablespoons soy sauce or tamari
- 1 tablespoon hoisin sauce
- 1 teaspoon grated fresh ginger
- 1 garlic clove, minced
- 1 tablespoon cornstarch mixed with 2 tablespoons water (for sauce thickening)
- Cooked brown rice or quinoa for serving
- Optional: sesame seeds or chopped green onions for garnish

Procedure:

- In a bowl, whisk together the soy sauce, hoisin sauce, grated ginger, and minced garlic to create the stir-fry sauce. Set aside.
- If using tofu or tempeh, heat a drizzle of oil in a large skillet or wok over medium-high heat. Add the cubed tofu or tempeh and cook until golden and crispy. Remove from the skillet and set aside.
- In the same skillet, heat another drizzle of oil over high heat.
- Sauté the sliced vegetables until crispy.
- If using tofu or tempeh, return it to the skillet with the vegetables.
- Pour the sauce over the vegetables and tofu.
- Push the tofu and vegetables to one side of the skillet and pour the cornstarch-water mixture into the open space.
- Quickly stir the mixture until it thickens into a glossy sauce.
- Gently combine the sauce with the tofu and vegetables, making sure everything is well coated.
- Remove from heat and serve the Magical Garden Veggie Stir-Fry over cooked brown rice or quinoa.
- Garnish with sesame seeds or chopped green onions if desired.
- Enjoy this enchanting veggie stir-fry that's bursting with colorful garden flavors!

CHEESY SPINACH STUFFED CHICKEN DAZZLE

Preparation Time: 30 minutes - Ingredients:

- 4 boneless, skinless chicken breasts
- 1 cup chopped fresh spinach
- 1/2 cup shredded mozzarella cheese
- 1/4 cup grated Parmesan cheese
- 1 garlic clove, minced
- Salt and pepper to taste
- 1 tablespoon olive oil
- Toothpicks (for securing the chicken)
- Optional: Italian seasoning for extra flavor

Procedure:

- Preheat the oven to 375°F (190°C).
- In a mixing bowl, combine the chopped fresh spinach, shredded mozzarella cheese, grated Parmesan cheese, minced garlic, salt, and pepper. Mix well to create the stuffing mixture.
- Crush the chicken slices to make them uniform.
- Place on each slice a tablespoon of the mixture.
- Roll up the chicken breasts, securing the ends with toothpicks to keep the stuffing inside.
- Heat the olive oil in an oven-safe skillet over medium-high heat.
- Sear the stuffed chicken breasts on all sides until they are golden brown, about 2-3 minutes per side.
- If desired, sprinkle Italian seasoning over the seared chicken breasts for extra flavor.
- Transfer the skillet to the preheated oven and bake for 15-20 minutes, or until the chicken is cooked through and no longer pink in the center.
- Remove the toothpicks from the chicken before serving.
- Serve the Cheesy Spinach Stuffed Chicken Dazzle with your favorite sides, such as roasted vegetables, mashed potatoes, or a crisp salad.

DIY VEGGIE TACOS WITH HOMEMADE SALSA

Preparation Time: 25 minutes - Ingredients:

For Veggie Tacos:

- 8 small corn or whole wheat tortillas
- 2 cups mixed vegetables (bell peppers, onions, zucchini, corn, etc.), sliced
- 1 cup black beans, drained and rinsed
- 1 cup cooked quinoa or brown rice
- 1 teaspoon chili powder
- 1/2 teaspoon cumin
- Salt and pepper to taste
- Olive oil for sautéing

For Homemade Salsa:

- 1 cup diced tomatoes
- 1/4 cup diced red onion
- 1/4 cup chopped fresh cilantro
- Juice of 1 lime
- Salt and pepper to taste

Procedure:

For Veggie Tacos:

- In a skillet, heat a drizzle of olive oil over medium heat.
- Add the vegetables in the pan and fry until caramelized.
- Add chili, black beans, cumin, a pinch of salt and pepper.
- Heat the tortillas on a non-stick pan.
- To assemble the tacos, spoon a portion of the cooked quinoa or brown rice onto each tortilla.
- Top with the sautéed veggie and black bean mixture.
- Garnish with your favorite toppings, such as shredded lettuce, diced avocado, and a dollop of homemade salsa.

For Homemade Salsa:

- In a bowl, combine the diced tomatoes, diced red onion, chopped cilantro, lime juice, salt, and pepper.
- Mix well to create a refreshing and tangy salsa.
- Serve the DIY Veggie Tacos with Homemade Salsa for a customizable dinner experience where everyone can build their own delicious and nutritious tacos.

CHAPTER 11
SNACKS
RECIPES

FRUITY PEBBLE YOGURT PARFAIT POPS

Preparation Time: 15 minutes (plus freezing time) - Ingredients:

- 1 cup Greek yogurt
- 1/2 cup mixed berries (strawberries, blueberries, raspberries), chopped
- 1/4 cup Fruity Pebbles cereal
- 2 tablespoons honey or maple syrup
- Popsicle molds or small cups
- Popsicle sticks

Procedure:

- In a bowl, mix the Greek yogurt and honey (or maple syrup) until well combined.
- Gently fold in the chopped mixed berries.
- Layer the yogurt mixture and Fruity Pebbles cereal in the popsicle molds or small cups, alternating between the two.
- Insert a popsicle stick into each mold.
- Place the molds in the freezer and let them freeze for at least 4 hours, or until the popsicles are completely frozen.
- Once frozen, remove the Fruity Pebble Yogurt Parfait Pops from the molds by running them briefly under warm water to loosen them.
- Enjoy these colorful and refreshing yogurt parfait pops as a delightful and fun snack!

MINI VEGGIE SUSHI ROLLS WITH DIPPING FUN

Preparation Time: 20 minutes - Ingredients:

- 4 nori seaweed sheets
- 1 cup sushi rice, cooked and seasoned with rice vinegar
- 1/2 cup mixed vegetables (cucumber, carrot, avocado, bell pepper), thinly sliced
- Soy sauce or tamari, for dipping
- Optional: sesame seeds for garnish
- Bamboo sushi rolling mat (makisu)

Procedure:

- Place a nori seaweed sheet.
- Then spread inside the rice.
- Lay the mixed vegetable slices horizontally across the center of the rice-covered nori.
- Starting from the edge closest to you, use the bamboo mat to tightly roll up the nori and rice around the vegetables, using gentle pressure.
- Wet the top edge of the nori to seal the roll.
- Repeat the process to create three more rolls.
- Use a sharp knife to slice each roll into bite-sized mini sushi rolls.
- Arrange the Mini Veggie Sushi Rolls on a serving plate.
- Sprinkle sesame seeds over the rolls for an extra burst of flavor and texture.
- Serve with a side of soy sauce or tamari for dipping.

CRUNCHY ROASTED CHICKPEA METEORITES

Preparation Time: 40 minutes - Ingredients:

- 1 can (15 oz) chickpeas (garbanzo beans), drained and rinsed
- 2 tablespoons olive oil
- 1 teaspoon ground cumin
- 1/2 teaspoon paprika
- 1/2 teaspoon garlic powder
- Salt and pepper to taste

Procedure:

- Preheat the oven to 400°F (200°C).
- Gently dry the chickpeas on a paper cloth.
- Put the chickpeas, olive oil, cumin, garlic powder, paprika and a pinch of salt and pepper in a bowl.
- Spread the seasoned chickpeas in a single layer on a baking sheet.
- Roast the chickpeas in the preheated oven for 30-35 minutes, or until they are golden brown and crispy, shaking the baking sheet occasionally to ensure even roasting.
- Remove the chickpeas from the oven and let them cool slightly before enjoying.

APPLE SLICE PENGUINS WITH NUTTY TUXEDOS

Preparation Time: 15 minutes - Ingredients:

- 1 apple
- Peanut butter or almond butter
- Mini chocolate chips
- Sliced almonds
- Edible googly eyes (or tiny pieces of white chocolate or yogurt drops)

Procedure:

- Wash and dry the apple.
- Slice the apple horizontally into rounds, about 1/4 inch thick.
- Spread a thin layer of peanut butter or almond butter on each apple slice.
- Place two mini chocolate chips near the top of each apple slice to create the penguins' eyes.
- Use two sliced almonds to create the penguins' arms, placing them on either side of the apple slice.
- Cut one more sliced almond in half to create the penguins' feet, placing them at the bottom of the slice.
- Optional: If using edible googly eyes, place them above the chocolate chip eyes.
- Place another mini chocolate chip on each apple slice to create the penguins' beaks.
- Arrange the Apple Slice Penguins on a serving plate, and watch them come to life!

CHEESY VEGGIE QUESADILLA POCKETS

Preparation Time: 15 minutes - Ingredients:

- 2 whole wheat tortillas
- 1/2 cup shredded cheddar cheese
- 1/4 cup mixed vegetables (bell peppers, onions, zucchini), diced
- 1/4 teaspoon ground cumin
- Salt and pepper to taste
- Cooking spray or olive oil

Procedure:

- In a bowl, combine the shredded cheddar cheese, diced mixed vegetables, ground cumin, salt, and pepper.
- Lay one whole wheat tortilla on a clean surface.
- Spoon the cheese and vegetable mixture onto half of the tortilla, leaving a border around the edges.
- Fold the other half of the tortilla over the filling to create a half-moon shape.
- Press down gently to seal the edges.
- Heat a non-stick skillet or griddle over medium heat and lightly grease it with cooking spray or a drizzle of olive oil.
- Place the quesadilla pocket on the skillet and cook until the tortilla is golden brown and the cheese is melted.
- Carefully remove the quesadilla pocket from the skillet and let it cool slightly before slicing it into wedges.

CHAPTER 12

BUILDING A CULINARY LEGACY

CHAPTER 12 - BUILDING A CULINARY LEGACY

'CAPTURING MEMORIES: DOCUMENTING YOUR CULINARY JOURNEY AND CREATIONS'

In the chapter titled "Capturing Memories: Documenting Your Culinary Journey and Creations," you'll learn how to turn your cooking adventures into a beautiful story that you can share with the world.

Creating Culinary Chronicles

Think of a chef's journal as your secret recipe book for memories. Just like a storyteller weaves tales, you'll weave your culinary journey into a narrative that's uniquely yours. Every recipe you try, every meal you make becomes a chapter in your culinary chronicles, a story of your growth and creativity.

Preserving Your Culinary Creations

Imagine the joy of flipping through pages filled with photos of your delicious dishes. A picture is worth a thousand words, and by capturing your culinary creations in photos, you're preserving memories that you can look back on with a smile. It's like bottling up the flavors and aromas of your dishes for future enjoyment.

Sharing Your Culinary Story

Your culinary journey is like a story waiting to be shared. Imagine the excitement of showing your family and friends the amazing dishes you've created. Whether it's through a photo album or a digital gallery, you'll take them on a journey through your culinary adventures, inspiring them to try new recipes and embrace their own creativity.

Building a Portfolio of Achievements

Imagine the sense of accomplishment as you flip through pages filled with your cooking triumphs. Just like an artist displays their paintings, you'll showcase your culinary achievements through photos. Whether it's a perfectly baked cake or a beautifully presented meal, your portfolio becomes a testament to your skills and dedication.

Capturing Special Moments

Cooking is not just about flavors; it's also about the memories you create. Imagine capturing the joy on your family's faces as they taste your delicious dishes. Whether it's a birthday celebration or a cozy dinner at home, your photos become a time capsule of special moments that you'll treasure forever.

Inspiring Others Through Your Journey

Your culinary journey is like an open book that inspires others to embark on their own cooking adventures. Imagine the impact you can make by sharing your photos and stories. As others see your growth and creativity, they'll be motivated to explore their own kitchen skills and create memories of their own.

Creating a Legacy

Imagine the legacy you'll leave behind as you document your culinary journey. Your photos become a window into your world, a way for future generations to glimpse your passion and creativity. Just like a historian preserves stories, you're preserving your culinary legacy for years to come.

Remember that capturing memories is like preserving the magic of your cooking adventures. Whether you're snapping a photo of a beautifully plated dish or documenting the steps of a new recipe, you're creating a visual record of your growth and creativity.

As you document your culinary journey, you're turning cooking into a story that's meant to be shared. Your photos become snapshots of joy, love, and deliciousness – a testament to your dedication and passion for cooking. So, grab your camera, capture those mouthwatering moments, and let your culinary story unfold through the pages of your chef's journal.

'PASSING ON THE PASSION: INSPIRING OTHERS TO EMBRACE THE ART OF COOKING'

You'll discover how your culinary skills can light up the lives of your friends, family, and even the world. It's like sharing a secret recipe for happiness that spreads smiles far and wide.

Cooking as a Gift

Think of your cooking as a special gift you can share with others. Just like a magician shares their tricks, you'll share your culinary creations and inspire those around you to embark on their own kitchen adventures. It's like giving the world a taste of your creativity and passion.

Creating Kitchen Magic Together

The joy of cooking with your friends and family by your side. When you cook together, you're not just making meals – you're creating memories that last a lifetime. Just like a team of superheroes, you'll work together to chop, stir, and season, turning ordinary ingredients into extraordinary dishes.

Inspiring Future Chefs

Your passion for cooking is like a spark that ignites the curiosity of others. Imagine the thrill of inspiring someone to step into the kitchen and give cooking a try. Whether it's teaching a sibling to make cookies or showing a friend how to flip pancakes, you're planting seeds of culinary curiosity that can blossom into lifelong skills.

Sharing Your Culinary Adventures

Taste the excitement of sharing your culinary journey with others. When you talk about your cooking adventures, you're not just recounting recipes – you're sharing stories of growth, creativity, and delicious discoveries. Just like a storyteller captivates their audience, you'll captivate your friends and family with tales from your kitchen.

Creating Connections Through Cooking

Cooking is like a language that brings people together. Imagine the joy of bonding with your loved ones as you cook and enjoy meals together. Whether it's a cozy dinner at home or a festive celebration, your cooking becomes a bridge that connects hearts and creates cherished moments.

Leading by Example

Look the impact you can make by leading with your passion. When others see your enthusiasm for cooking, they'll be inspired to embrace the art of cooking themselves. You're like a guide who lights up the path for others, showing them that cooking is not just a chore – it's a journey of creativity and joy.

Spreading Happiness, One Dish at a Time

Cooking is like spreading happiness on a plate. As you inspire others to cook, you're not just sharing recipes – you're sharing joy, love, and a sense of accomplishment. Every dish you create becomes an invitation for others to experience the magic of cooking.

That your passion for cooking has the power to inspire others. Whether you're teaching a friend to make their first omelet or sharing your culinary adventures with your family, you're creating ripples of inspiration that touch hearts and ignite curiosity.

So, put on your apron, gather your loved ones, and let your passion for cooking be the spark that ignites a culinary revolution of inspiration and happiness!

CHAPTER 13
REAL STORIES, REAL CHEFS

CHAPTER 13 - REAL STORIES, REAL CHEFS

'INSPIRING JOURNEYS: STORIES OF YOUNG CHEFS WHO OVERCAME CHALLENGES AND FOUND SUCCESS'

In this chapter you'll meet fellow culinary adventurers who faced challenges head-on and emerged as shining stars in the kitchen. The different stories will show you what you can do with a little imagination, will and confidence in the kitchen.

Meet the Culinary Heroes

Think of these young chefs as your kitchen superheroes – they've faced obstacles and transformed them into stepping stones to success. Their journeys are like exciting tales filled with twists, turns, and delicious triumphs. From baking blunders to recipe rescues, their stories will inspire you to believe in your own culinary magic.

Turning Challenges into Opportunities

Learning how these young chefs turned their challenges into opportunities for growth. Just like a problem solver cracks codes, they cracked the code of turning mishaps into lessons. Their stories will teach you that setbacks are not roadblocks – they're chances to learn, adapt, and become better chefs.

Finding Passion in Every Dish

These young chefs are like artists who paint with flavors. Imagine the joy they feel as they create dishes that reflect their passion and personality. Whether it's a cake that tells a story or a savory dish that's a burst of creativity, their culinary masterpieces are a testament to their dedication and love for cooking.

Embracing Creativity and Individuality

Imagine discovering how these young chefs added their unique twist to classic recipes. Just like an inventor designs new gadgets, they've designed dishes that showcase their creativity. Their stories will show you that cooking is not just following a recipe – it's about infusing every dish with your personal touch.

Celebrating Success, One Recipe at a Time

These young chefs are like champions who celebrate every victory – big or small. Imagine the satisfaction they feel as they present their dishes to the world. Whether it's a perfectly baked pie or a beautifully plated meal, their stories remind us that success is a journey, and every recipe conquered is a step closer to greatness.

Learning from Setbacks

Imagine the resilience these young chefs demonstrated when faced with setbacks. Just like an explorer finds a way through uncharted territories, they found a way to overcome challenges and keep moving forward. Their stories will teach you that setbacks are not defeats – they're opportunities to learn and improve.

Inspiring Your Own Journey

These young chefs' stories are like a roadmap that guides you on your own culinary journey. Imagine the inspiration you'll feel as you read about their challenges, successes, and delicious creations. Their stories will motivate you to set your own goals, tackle challenges, and create your own culinary story.

As you read their inspiring stories, you'll realize that the world of cooking is filled with endless possibilities. Whether you dream of becoming a baking maestro or a culinary innovator, these young chefs' stories will show you that the journey is as important as the destination.

So, grab your apron, gather your ingredients, and let the stories of these culinary heroes be your guiding light on your own delicious adventure!

'CONNECTING THROUGH COOKING: BUILDING A COMMUNITY OF YOUNG CULINARY ENTHUSIASTS'

Would you like to experience the joy of being part of a community that celebrates creativity, friendship and delicious food? It is like entering a club where each member speaks the language of flavors and spices.

Cooking as a Common Bond

Think of this community as a gathering of friends who all have one thing in common – their love for cooking. Just like a puzzle, you'll fit right in, connecting with others who share your passion for creating mouthwatering dishes. It's like finding your culinary tribe, where everyone understands the magic that happens in the kitchen.

Sharing Recipes and Ideas

Whether it's a pancake recipe you've perfected or a new twist on a classic dish, you'll exchange ideas and culinary creations that inspire each other. It's like a recipe swap where everyone contributes to the deliciousness.

Inspiring and Being Inspired

Being part of a community means not just sharing your creations but also getting inspired by others. Imagine discovering new ingredients, techniques, and flavor combinations from fellow young chefs. It's like having a recipe book that's constantly growing, filled with ideas that ignite your culinary curiosity.

Learning and Growing Together

Just like a team, you'll tackle challenges, celebrate successes, and support each other's culinary journeys. It's like having friends who encourage you to step out of your comfort zone and try new recipes, techniques, and flavors.

Cooking Challenges and Contests

Imagine the thrill of participating in cooking challenges and contests within the community. Whether it's a baking showdown or a creativity challenge, these events are like exciting games that test your culinary skills. It's like joining a friendly competition where everyone's a winner because they've grown and learned through the experience.

Making Friends Around the World

Being part of a community means making friends from different corners of the globe. Imagine connecting with young chefs from different cultures, each with their own culinary traditions and stories to share. It's like embarking on a culinary journey that expands your horizons and brings the world to your kitchen.

Spreading Positive Vibes

Whether it's a perfectly risen cake or a beautifully plated dish, you'll spread smiles and encouragement like confetti.

Being part of a community of young culinary enthusiasts means you're surrounded by friends who share your passion and creativity. Together, you'll cook up a storm, exchange ideas, and inspire each other to reach new culinary heights.

As you connect through cooking, you'll discover that food is not just nourishment – it's a way to build friendships, create memories, and spread joy. Whether you're sharing recipes, competing in challenges, or simply chatting about your latest kitchen triumphs, you're building connections that will last a lifetime. Join the community, and let the world of young chefs be your playground of friendship, creativity, and delicious adventures!

CHAPTER 14

YOUR CULINARY ADVENTURE AWAITS

CHAPTER 14 - YOUR CULINARY ADVENTURE AWAITS

'BEYOND THE BOOK: EXPLORING FURTHER RESOURCES, BLOGS, AND ONLINE COMMUNITIES'

Be ready to discover a treasure trove of online wonders that will take your culinary journey to exciting new heights. It's like opening a secret door that leads to a magical world of culinary exploration.

The Joy of Online Exploration

Think of the internet as a giant playground just waiting for you to explore. Just like an explorer embarks on adventures, you'll venture into the online realm to find blogs, websites, and communities filled with cooking tips, recipes, and culinary inspiration. It's like having a library of cooking knowledge at your fingertips.

Learning from Experts

Try learning from chefs, food experts, and fellow young culinary enthusiasts who share their wisdom online. Just like a student learns from their teachers, you'll learn from those who are passionate about cooking and eager to share their knowledge. Their insights and tips will be like little gems that enhance your cooking skills.

Discovering New Recipes

Imagine stumbling upon a treasure trove of new and exciting recipes that you've never heard of before. Whether it's a fusion dish that blends flavors from different cuisines or a dessert that looks like a work of art, you'll discover recipes that tickle your taste buds and ignite your creativity.

Exploring Online Communities

Being part of online communities is like joining a club of like-minded young chefs. Imagine connecting with others who share your love for cooking, exchanging ideas, and sharing your culinary triumphs. It's like having friends from all over the world who understand your passion and speak your culinary language.

Getting Inspired by Blogs

Blogs are like windows into the world of cooking. Imagine reading stories of cooking adventures, discovering kitchen hacks, and finding inspiration in the culinary journeys of others. Just like a storyteller captivates their audience, bloggers captivate your imagination with their words and experiences.

Joining Cooking Challenges

It's a challenge to create a dish using specific ingredients or a theme that sparks your creativity, these challenges are like puzzles that test your skills and reward you with culinary satisfaction.

Learning at Your Own Pace

The beauty of online resources is that you can learn at your own pace. Imagine having the freedom to explore, practice, and experiment whenever you want. Whether you're a beginner or an aspiring young chef, you'll find resources that match your skill level and curiosity.

Beyond the pages of your cookbook, there's a universe of blogs, websites, and online communities waiting for you to dive in. From learning new techniques to discovering unique recipes, these resources are like hidden gems that will make your culinary journey even more exciting and fulfilling.

As you explore further resources, blogs, and online communities, you'll realize that cooking is not just about following recipes – it's a continuous journey of discovery, creativity, and growth. Open your browser, and let the world of online culinary exploration be your guide to endless possibilities!

'CULINARY EXPLORATION: EMBARKING ON NEW ADVENTURES IN THE WORLD OF COOKING'

Unveiling the Magic of Ingredients

Think of ingredients as the stars of your culinary adventure. Just like a treasure hunter seeks hidden gems, you'll explore the flavors, textures, and aromas of each ingredient to create mouthwatering dishes. It's like opening a door to a magical world where tomatoes can be sweet, sour, or even umami.

Experimenting with Flavors

Imagine combining different ingredients to create flavor combinations that surprise and delight your taste buds. Just like an artist mixes colors to create a masterpiece, you'll mix flavors to create dishes that are uniquely yours. It's like composing a symphony of tastes that dance on your palate.

Exploring Cultural Cuisines

Cuisines from around the world are like windows into different cultures. Imagine traveling to far-off lands through your taste buds, experiencing the spices, herbs, and traditions of different countries. It's like embarking on a culinary adventure that expands your horizons and introduces you to new ways of cooking and eating.

Trying New Techniques

Imagine mastering cooking techniques that turn ordinary ingredients into extraordinary dishes. Whether it's sautéing, grilling, or baking, you'll learn to wield kitchen tools like a wizard wielding a wand. It's like adding new spells to your culinary repertoire, each one enhancing your cooking magic.

Creating Your Signature Dishes

Imagine the pride of creating dishes that reflect your personality and culinary style. Just like an inventor creates new gadgets, you'll create recipes that are uniquely yours. From adding a special twist to a classic recipe to inventing a dish that's never been seen before, you'll leave your mark on the world of cooking.

Elevating Everyday Meals

Every meal can be an opportunity for culinary exploration. Imagine turning everyday ingredients into extraordinary dishes that surprise and delight your family and friends. It's like sprinkling a dash of creativity onto your meals, transforming them into memorable dining experiences.

Learning from Mistakes

Imagine the wisdom you gain from kitchen mishaps and mistakes. Just like a detective solves mysteries, you'll solve the puzzle of what went wrong and learn how to avoid it next time. It's like turning setbacks into stepping stones that lead you to culinary excellence.

With every recipe you try, every ingredient you explore, and every technique you master, you're adding to your treasure trove of cooking knowledge and experience. It's like writing your own culinary story, one dish at a time.

You'll discover that cooking is not just a task – it's a joyful journey of discovery, creativity, and growth. Let the magic of culinary exploration guide you to new horizons of deliciousness and wonder!

CONCLUSION

EMBRACING YOUR ROLE AS A YOUNG CHEF: LOOKING BACK AND MOVING FORWARD WITH CONFIDENCE

CONCLUSION - EMBRACING YOUR ROLE AS A YOUNG CHEF: LOOKING BACK AND MOVING FORWARD WITH CONFIDENCE

As you reach the final chapter of your culinary journey, take a moment to reflect on how far you've come. In the chapter titled "Embracing Your Role as a Young Chef: Looking Back and Moving Forward with Confidence," you'll celebrate your accomplishments, appreciate your growth, and step forward with newfound culinary confidence. It's like standing at the finish line of a race you've run with passion and determination.

Celebrating Your Achievements

Imagine looking back at the recipes you've conquered, the techniques you've mastered, and the flavors you've explored. Just like a hero celebrates their victories, you'll celebrate your culinary achievements – big and small. It's like receiving a medal for every delicious dish you've created.

Gaining Confidence

Remember the first time you entered the kitchen? Now look at how you've blossomed into a young chef with skills and creativity. Just like a caterpillar transforms into a butterfly, you've transformed into a culinary artist who can whip up magic with a whisk and a sprinkle of imagination.

Building Lifelong Skills

Think of cooking as a superpower you've acquired. Just like a superhero hones their abilities, you've honed your cooking skills, turning ordinary ingredients into extraordinary creations. It's like having a tool that lets you nourish yourself and your loved ones with deliciousness and love.

Embracing Challenges

Remember the times when a recipe seemed like a puzzle you couldn't solve? Now look at how you've faced challenges head-on and triumphed. Just like an explorer conquers mountains, you've conquered kitchen obstacles and emerged stronger, wiser, and even more eager to learn.

Creating Memories

Think of all the meals you've cooked and shared with family and friends. Each dish is like a brushstroke on the canvas of your culinary journey. Just like an artist creates paintings that tell stories, you've created meals that have brought joy, laughter, and togetherness to the table.

Spreading Joy Through Food

Imagine the smiles and satisfied bellies of those who've tasted your creations. Just like a magician spreads wonder with their tricks, you've spread joy and happiness through the magic of your cooking. It's like sharing a piece of your heart with every bite.

Looking Ahead with Confidence

As you close this chapter and open the door to the future, know that your culinary journey is just beginning. Imagine the endless possibilities that await you – new recipes to try, new techniques to master, and new flavors to explore. Just like an explorer sets sail to new lands, you'll set out to new culinary horizons with confidence and excitement.

So, as you close the book on this culinary adventure, remember that you're not just closing a chapter – you're opening a new one filled with opportunities, growth, and delicious discoveries. Your journey as a young chef is a story of determination, passion, and creative flair. It's like a recipe that's uniquely yours, crafted with love and dedication.

As you move forward, embrace your role as a young chef with pride. Your kitchen is your canvas, and your ingredients are your colors. All the dishes you cook, represent a new story and a new adventure in the world of cooking, roll up your sleeves, put on your chef's hat and start to become the best cook you can be. You're not just a young chef – you're a culinary artist with a world of flavors at your fingertips!

Made in United States
Troutdale, OR
12/29/2023